T0357934

She's *on the* Money
budget journal

Victoria Devine is transforming the way millennials think about money. With a background in behavioural psychology and a chart-topping podcast, *She's on the Money*, Victoria understands what makes her generation tick and she knows how to make hard-to-understand concepts fun, fresh and relatable.

Now retired from her role as an award-winning financial adviser, Victoria continues to be a co-director and founder of Zella Money, an award-winning mortgage-broking business. She has been a guest speaker at events and featured in publications such as *The Financial Standard*, *Vogue*, ABC News, RMIT Future of Financial Planning, Mamamia, *Elle* magazine, Yahoo Finance and many more. She was also named on the *Forbes* 30 Under 30 Asia list for 2021.

Victoria's number one bestselling first book, *She's on the Money*, won the ABIA General Non-fiction Book of the Year 2022 and the Best Personal Finance & Investment Book of the Year at the 2021 Business Book Awards.

If you can't find her, chances are she's at home with an oat latte in one hand and her Old English Sheepadoodle, Lucy, in the other.

shesonthemoney.com.au
@shesonthemoneyaus
@ShesontheMoneyAUS

Also by Victoria Devine

She's on the Money
Investing with She's on the Money

She's *on the* Money
budget journal

*Today is the day to change
your financial future*

Victoria Devine

PENGUIN LIFE

UK | USA | Canada | Ireland | Australia
India | New Zealand | South Africa | China

Penguin Life is part of the Penguin Random House group of companies
whose addresses can be found at global.penguinrandomhouse.com.

Penguin
Random House
Australia

First published by Penguin Life in 2023

Cover design © Penguin Random House Australia Pty Ltd
Author photograph by Miranda Stokke
Printed and bound in Australia by Griffin Press,
an accredited ISO AS/NZS 14001 Environmental Management Systems printer.

 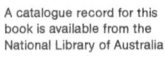 A catalogue record for this
book is available from the
National Library of Australia

ISBN 978 1 76134 142 7

penguin.com.au

We at Penguin Random House Australia acknowledge that Aboriginal and Torres Strait Islander peoples
are the Traditional Custodians and the first storytellers of the lands on which we live and work. We honour
Aboriginal and Torres Strait Islander peoples' continuous connection to Country, waters, skies and communities.
We celebrate Aboriginal and Torres Strait Islander stories, traditions and living cultures;
and we pay our respects to Elders past and present.

**The information in this book is of a general nature only and does not take into account your financial
situation, objectives or needs. The information has been compiled from sources considered to be reliable
at the time of publication, but not guaranteed. Before acting on any of this information, you should
consider its appropriateness to your own financial situation, objectives and needs.**

Contents

"

reality

Make your
dreams a

"

Hello Friend!

I'm so excited to have created this journal for you. As you know, She's on the Money is all about helping you take control of your financial mindset and habits so you can realise your ideal Future You. While there's tons of info in the *She's on the Money* podcast and books, I wanted to give you this personal space to plan and track your unique journey. It's jam-packed with planners, tips, inspiration and check-ins to guide your goals and track your progress.

While you don't need any extra materials, if you're ever keen on a deeper dive into some of the things we cover here, the book series has your back, including a 12-month action plan that might be fun to play along with as you complete your monthly reviews.

I hope working through this journal gives you the daily support you need to help your money dreams come true.

Victoria x

"

done
is better
than perfect

"

Be a goal getter

As I often say, 'I believe we can achieve everything. Just not all at once.' But the best way to reach your future dreams is to break them down into achievable goals.

We like using the She's on the Money framework to ensure our goals are: Specific, Optimistic, Time-bound and Measurable. The magic number of goals I like to focus on is five: one long-term (up to 10 years), two medium-term (3–5 years) and two short-term (within 12 months).

Seemingly small savings today can become huge gains over time and this section gives you all the tools you need to dream big. So, get brainstorming and start planning your Future You awaits!

Set your SOTM goals

- Imagine Future You. Where do you want to be in 5–10 years?
- Think about what you need to achieve financially in 10 years, 3–5 years and 12 months, to get there.
- In the pages ahead, write these up as your long-term, medium-term and short-term goals.
- Being flexible is important, so reassess your goals often, as your life and priorities change.
- Your goals should follow the She's on the Money framework to make them:
  Specific, Optimistic, Time-bound and Measurable.

SOTM goals

SPECIFIC (S)

Your goals need to be clear and specific, otherwise you won't be able to focus your efforts or truly feel motivated to achieve them. The more specific the better – choose an exact figure for your savings goal, set an exact time frame to reach it, and include specific details (e.g. colour, shape, location) about your dream object. Write down the details of your goal using active verbs to describe it, i.e. 'I will save $10,000 before the end of the year', instead of 'I would like to save $10,000 before the end of the year.'

OPTIMISTIC (O)

If your goals don't match your values, it'll be mighty hard to stick to them – while I want you to be realistic, I also want you to be optimistic. You might think you can't break old spending habits or ever earn enough to invest in shares or property, but by paying attention to your money story and spending behaviours, you can start to change the patterns that are holding you back. Changing just one of your spending habits can save thousands over the long-term. It's truly amazing what's possible!

Set your SOTM goals

TIME-BOUND (T)

T

All the goals you set need to have a target date to make sure you've got a deadline to focus on. Keep these dates in relevant areas, put them into your calendar or diary and include reminders each month so you know when your dates are coming up. This way you can track your progress on a regular basis – celebrate successes along the way, or make changes to your plan if you've gone a bit off track.

MEASURABLE (M)

M

Measurable goals allow you to clearly chart your progress, stay on track and stay motivated. Using precise figures or numbers means you know when you're about to cross the finish line and when to celebrate the completion of a goal. Being able to measure where you're currently at helps you stay focused after the initial excitement and motivation of goal setting has worn off. Actively measuring your progress also allows you to reassess, e.g. if you're three months into a six-month goal, are you still on track? Or do you need to work a little bit harder to make sure you're still going to achieve what you set out to?

Long-term goals

A long-term goal can take up to 10 years to achieve.

Non-specific goal: *I want* To buy a house.

Now let's break down the goal using the SOTM framework to make it more achievable.

MY *Specific* GOAL IS	I will save enough money for a house deposit in Melbourne.
IS THIS GOAL *Optimistic* AND REALISTIC?	I will save $20,000 for a house deposit on an $800,000 house in Melbourne, so that my partner and I can start The process of looking for a new home and planning for our future family goals.
WHAT IS MY *Target* DATE?	I will save $20,000 for a house deposit in just over 3 years (40 months), by January 2026.
I WILL *Measure* THIS GOAL BY	After completing my monthly budget, I can save $2,000 per month for a house deposit. I will track my progress: after one year I should have $24,000 saved and after Two years I should have $48,000 saved.

MY *SOTM* LONG-TERM FINANCIAL GOAL IS:

I will save $20,000 for a house deposit on a $800,000 home in Melbourne by January 2026 by putting $2,000 per month Towards it. Once I have completed This goal, my partner and I will be able To start The process of looking for our new home and planning for our future family goals.

Medium-term goals

A medium-term goal takes 3–5 years to achieve.

Non-specific goal: _I want to travel overseas._

Now let's break down the goal using the SOTM framework to make it more achievable.

MY *Specific* GOAL IS	I want to have a European summer holiday.
IS THIS GOAL *Optimistic* AND REALISTIC?	I would like to holiday for 4–6 weeks in Italy during the European summer. I must save enough to cover airfares, food, accommodation and spending money.
WHAT IS MY *Target* DATE?	I will save $6,000 over 18 months, so I can holiday for 4 weeks in Italy during July–August 2025.
I WILL *Measure* THIS GOAL BY	I will achieve my goal of $6,000 by saving $333.50 per month. After six months I should have $2,000 saved and after 12 months I should have $4,000 saved.

MY *SOTM* MEDIUM-TERM FINANCIAL GOAL IS:

I will save $6,000 for a summer holiday in Italy in 2025, by saving $333.50 per month for the next 18 months.

During this time I will also shop in ways that can help me accrue frequent flyer points which I can use towards my flights and I will keep an eye out for cheap fares so I can put more towards enjoying the holiday itself.

Short-Term goals

A short-term goal is a goal you can achieve in 12 months or less.

Non-specific goal: *I want to be debt free.*

Now let's break it down using the SOTM framework to make it more achievable.

MY *Specific* GOAL IS	*I will pay off my $3,000 credit card debt in full.*
IS THIS GOAL *Optimistic* AND REALISTIC?	*I will pay off my credit card debt in full so I can reallocate the payment funds to setting up my emergency fund and gaining financial freedom.*
WHAT IS MY *Target* DATE?	*I will pay off my $3,000 credit card debt in full in 10 months, by the end of July next year.*
I WILL *Measure* THIS GOAL BY	*To successfully pay off my $3,000 debt, I will put $300 plus interest every month towards my credit card. I will also stop using my credit card to avoid accumulating additional debt.*

MY *SOTM* SHORT-TERM FINANCIAL GOAL IS:

I will pay off my $3,000 credit card debt in full by the end of July next year by putting $300 per month plus interest towards it and not using my card during this time. By completing this goal, I will be able to reallocate the payment funds to setting up my emergency fund and gaining financial freedom.

Long-term goal

A long-term goal can take up to 10 years to achieve.

Non-specific goal:

Now let's break down the goal using the SOTM framework to make it more achievable.

MY *Specific* GOAL IS	
IS THIS GOAL *Optimistic* AND REALISTIC?	
WHAT IS MY *Target* DATE?	
I WILL *Measure* THIS GOAL BY	

MY *SOTM* LONG-TERM FINANCIAL GOAL IS:

Medium-term goal!

A medium-term goal takes 3–5 years to achieve.

Non-specific goal: _____

Now let's break the goal down using the SOTM framework to make it more achievable.

MY *Specific* GOAL IS	
IS THIS GOAL *Optimistic* AND REALISTIC?	
WHAT IS MY *Target* DATE?	
I WILL *Measure* THIS GOAL BY	

MY *SOTM* MEDIUM-TERM FINANCIAL GOAL IS:

_____

_____

_____

_____

Medium-term goal 2

A medium-term goal takes 3–5 years to achieve.

Non-specific goal: _____

Now let's break the goal down using the SOTM framework to make it more achievable.

MY *Specific* GOAL IS _____

IS THIS GOAL *Optimistic* AND REALISTIC? _____

WHAT IS MY *Target* DATE? _____

I WILL *Measure* THIS GOAL BY _____

MY *SOTM* MEDIUM-TERM FINANCIAL GOAL IS:

_____

_____

_____

_____

Short-term goal!

A short-term goal is a goal you can achieve in 12 months or less.

Non-specific goal: _____

Now, let's break the goal down using the SOTM framework to make it more achievable.

MY *Specific* GOAL IS

IS THIS GOAL *Optimistic* AND REALISTIC?

WHAT IS MY *Target* DATE?

I WILL *Measure* THIS GOAL BY

MY *SOTM* SHORT-TERM FINANCIAL GOAL IS:

Short-Term goal 2

A short-term goal is a goal you can achieve in 12 months or less.

Non-specific goal: _____

Now, let's break the goal down using the SOTM framework to make it more achievable.

MY *Specific* GOAL IS	
IS THIS GOAL *Optimistic* AND REALISTIC?	
WHAT IS MY *Target* DATE?	
I WILL *Measure* THIS GOAL BY	

MY *SOTM* SHORT-TERM FINANCIAL GOAL IS:

_____

_____

_____

_____

"

Does it

align

with your
values?

"

Setting up right

My first book, *She's on the Money*, featured a whole chapter on cash flow and wrapped up with a 12-month action plan. Here, I include some practical tools and resources to help you flow your money into the right buckets and set budgets that work for your personal spending needs. And yes! they can (and should) include some fun stuff for you too, not to mention gifts for friends and family. What's more, if you organise yourself up front, even tax time can be a breeze.

Setting yourself up right in the first place helps these habits become easier to stick with. So first, let's take a look at your cash flow and then start planning your magnificent year ahead.

Let's map out your money

The first step towards financial freedom is figuring out what you earn, spend, own and owe.

While you may know these figures off the top of your head, it is handy to have access to your bank account, pay slips and/or credit card statement.

Write down your monthly numbers

EARN	This is any income that comes into your bank account in a month. This may come from salary, side hustle, investment or allowance. If your earnings vary each month, write down the lowest amount you would earn on average.	*Earn*
SPEND	This is any money that goes out of your bank account in a month from rent, to food, to bills and bank fees. It's okay if this is an average as we will get a more accurate figure as you complete this budget journal.	*Spend*
OWN	What you own is important because that's what's going to create your net wealth. This includes how much you have in your superannuation account, whether you own a property (and how much it's worth) and if you have any assets or savings accounts – essentially, anything that could be sold for monetary value or that produces an income.	*Own*
OWE	This is any debt you have, good or bad, such as a personal loan, HELP/HECS debt, credit card debt or a mortgage.	*Owe*

Now that you have your four numbers, how do they look? Are you spending more than you earn? Breaking even? Rolling in extra cash?

Your foolproof cash-flow funnel

There are many ways to break down your budget, but I find the easiest (and most successful) is to set up a foolproof funnel that will keep your cash going exactly where it needs to. I've developed this system that can work for anyone on any income and at any stage of life. I'm not going to tell you what percentage should be allocated to each of these funnels, because everyone's financial position is different. Simply look at your capacity, make sure you're staying true to your goals and values, and then decide what you can realistically maintain. Be sure to review, too, if your circumstances change through the year.

All income

CASH HUB ACCOUNT

All income banked into a single account. Total amount coming into this account:

WEEKLY SPENDING ACCOUNT

A nominated amount deposited via direct debit every week on a day of your choice.

Spending money for:
• food
• fuel
• fun etc.

Total amount coming into this account:

NOT AN EMERGENCY BUT IT FEELS LIKE AN EMERGENCY ACCOUNT

Transfer any leftover weekly spending money to this account.

BILLS AND FIXED COSTS

All paid via direct debit or BPAY directly from your cash hub.

Things like:
• phone/internet
• health insurance
• rent
• subscriptions

Total amount coming out of this account:

EMERGENCY FUND

Total amount coming into this account:

SHORT-TERM SAVINGS ACCOUNT

Total amount coming into this account:

MEDIUM-TO-LONG TERM SAVINGS ACCOUNT

Total amount coming into this account:

INVESTMENT GOALS

If you have begun your investment journey, you'll want to ensure that it's accounted for on your cash flow plan. Total amount allocated towards investment:

Challenge!

Break down your yearly expenses into monthly amounts
so you can prepare for and manage them year round!

BILL	TOTAL AMOUNT (APPROX.)	MONTHLY COST (TOTAL/12)
Insurances		
Travel costs		
Credit card fees		
Tax preparation fees		
TOTAL		

Remember to include the total monthly cost for these annual expenses
in your monthly budget forecasts, which you'll begin in Quarter 1.
If you're following the foolproof cash-flow funnel,
these amounts should be directed to your cash hub.

Money Tip!

Spend time every year *reassessing* your bills.

You may find a power company, insurance provider or phone plan that offers welcome credits or lower fees.

Big moments budget

Later, in the detailed monthly budgets, you'll take a closer look at regular bills and recurring payments. But life also comes with its big moments, right? – arguably the most important, and usually, the most fun – especially when you've planned ahead so you can enjoy them without feeling stressed! Add your big moments to the table below, use the prompts beneath to figure out your average spend, then create an adjusted (more realistic) budget for each event based on its importance. Dividing the total budget by 12 will give you a guide as to how much you need to set aside into your short-term savings account each month to cover these costs.

Big moments planning

BIG MOMENT	BUDGET
My birthday	$700

TOTAL BUDGET: _____

TOTAL NUMBER OF BIG MOMENTS: _____

To work out your average budget per moment, divide total budget by number of big moments.

total budget/number of big moments = $ _____

To work out how much money you should set aside in savings each month, divide total budget by 12.

total budget/12 = $ _____

Big moment budget

Big moment : *My birthday*

Total budget $ 700

Big moment spending doesn't just get out of hand because of the gifts we purchase.
Money seemingly walks straight out of our wallets as we spend it on food, parties, outfits and
travel expenses. First, list all the things you think you might need to budget for in the table,
then in the space below, think about ways you could save on big and little items.
Bank any wins into your savings for Future You to enjoy.

Actual spend

ITEM	BUDGETED	ACTUAL	DIFFERENCE
A new outfit	$300	$150	+ $150
Venue hire	$150	$0	+ $150
Catering	$250	$250	+ $0
TOTAL			+ $300

Ways to save

Hire a dress for the night

Host at home

Ask guests to bring a plate

Big moment budget

Big moment: _____

Total budget $ _____

Big moment spending doesn't just get out of hand because of the gifts we purchase.
Money seemingly walks straight out of our wallets as we spend it on food, parties, outfits and
travel expenses. First, list all the things you think you might need to budget for in the table,
then in the space below, think about ways you could save on big and little items.
Bank any wins into your savings for Future You to enjoy.

Actual spend

ITEM	BUDGETED	ACTUAL	DIFFERENCE
TOTAL			

Ways to save

_____

_____

_____

_____

Big moment budget

Big moment: _____

Total budget $ _____

Big moment spending doesn't just get out of hand because of the gifts we purchase. Money seemingly walks straight out of our wallets as we spend it on food, parties, outfits and travel expenses. First, list all the things you think you might need to budget for in the table, then in the space below, think about ways you could save on big and little items. Bank any wins into your savings for future you to enjoy.

Actual spend

ITEM	BUDGETED	ACTUAL	DIFFERENCE
TOTAL			

Ways to save

_____

_____

_____

_____

Festive season budget

It's all well and good to say that we want to budget better for the holidays, but that is almost impossible without a plan. It's no surprise to any of us that the holidays are an extremely expensive time of the year. Keep track of your festive season budget by tracking gifts, parties and those extra choccies you pick up on the way to Aunt Mary's because you forgot a gift.

Gift planning

Budget

NAME	GIFT IDEA	COST	WAYS I COULD SAVE
Aunt Mary	Box of chocolates	$20	Make cookies

OVERALL BUDGET:

TOTAL NUMBER OF GIFTS TO BUY:

OVERALL BUDGET/TOTAL NUMBER OF GIFTS = BUDGET PER GIFT

I will spend no more than $_____ on each gift for the holidays

Challenge!

Create a specific savings goal and map it out using the grid below. Divide the goal by 100
(each square is worth that much). As you save, colour in the squares.

My Goal: $ _____

	EACH SQUARE = $ _____ /100 = $ _____
25% DONE $ _____	75% DONE $ _____
50% DONE $ _____	⭐ WELL DONE!

Start:

[Grid of squares with the following coloured cells:]
- 25% (light grey square)
- 50% (medium grey square)
- 75% (dark grey square)
- ⭐ (dark square with star)

Yay! You did it.

Tax-time Tips

There are many resources online where you can find what you can and can't claim
at tax time (check out the ATO website for the full and most up-to-date list).
Here are some examples to keep in mind when tracking these purchases!

What might you be able to claim?

COMMON WORK-RELATED EXPENSES	• Vehicle and travel expenses (this is only valid if you use your car for work purposes, and generally does not include daily travel to and from work). • Work-related clothing and laundry expenses, e.g. specific uniforms with a company logo that you are required to wear, personal protective equipment (PPE) and occupation-specific clothing. • Self-education expenses (where the course directly relates to your income).
OTHER WORK-RELATED EXPENSES	• Working from home expenses (there are a few different ways to work this out depending on how often you work from home, so check with your tax agent or the ATO website to work out which way to claim). • Phone, data and internet expenses (check that this isn't already claimed in your work from home expenses). • Tools, equipment and other assets used to perform your work duties, e.g. computers and software, desks and chairs, bookshelves, hand tools, safety equipment. • Union fees and subscriptions to trade, business or professional associations. • There are also a number of occupation and industry specific deductions which you can check out on the ATO website.

Tax-time tips

What might you be able to claim?

OTHER EXPENSES

- The cost of managing your tax affairs from the previous year, i.e. if you paid for a tax agent to lodge your tax return last year, you can claim that cost in your tax return this year.
- Gifts and donations (check that these are tax deductible).
- Interest, dividend and other investment income deductions, e.g. account-keeping fees on an account held for investment purposes.
- The cost of premiums you pay for income protection insurance (not available if your income protection insurance is taken out through your insurance).

What can't you claim?

- Cost of general household items like coffee, tea and milk.
- General clothing.
- Childcare.
- Any work-related expense that your employer has paid for or reimbursed you for.

Tax-time tips

Let's say you receive a tax return when tax time comes around (good for you!).
Other than purchasing that handbag you've been eyeing off, what are some other ways
you could allocate the money you get back?

- Make a contribution to your super.
- Pop it into your savings account, or a savings account for your children.
- Pay off credit card debt or loans.
- Put it into a mortgage offset account.
- Add it to your emergency fund.
- Add it to your yearly expenses account.
- Invest in shares.
- Invest in your personal growth through a hobby or a course (even better if it's a course that relates to your profession and may be deductible in next year's tax return!).
- Donate to a cause that's close to your heart.
- Treat yourself to a nice dinner or day out (after you've done one of the above!).

Be sure to research and consider the consequences of various ideas such as these -
it might be handy to refer back to my books to do just that!

This year, I am going to allocate my tax return as follows:

1. _____

2. _____

3. _____

4. _____

5. _____

Tax claims purchases Tracker

Remember, you need to keep records for expenses when you claim a deduction.
So hang on to those receipts!

DATE	DESCRIPTION	CATEGORY	AMOUNT

Know your

worth

then add tax

Quarter 1

Now, it's time to start getting into the nitty gritty – we'll drill down from a quarterly, to a monthly, to a daily view, so you can set yourself up right from the get-go and track your progress easily throughout the year. This first quarter's materials include examples on how to fill out each sheet, so check back here if ever you need a refresher.

You'll start by forecasting your monthly costs, then tracking your daily spending during the month, and finally, comparing your actual spend against your forecast. At the end of each month, there's room to consider your money wins and confessions.

If you're playing along with the 12-month action plan from the book, *She's on the Money*, here are the first three months' activities.

Month 1: Money story and budgeting
Month 2: Goal setting and money mapping
Month 3: Find your experts

Monthly budget forecast

Complete these pages at the beginning of each month to
forecast what your expenses will be. If you need a refresher,
I run through fixed/necessary expenses and variable/discretionary
expenses in Chapter 2 of *She's on the Money*.

MONTH: *February*	YEAR: *2023*

Income

SOURCE	GROSS	TAX	NET
Salary	*$5,833.33*	*$1,222.00*	*$4,611.33*
Side hustle	*$2,500.00*	*$589.00*	*$1,911.00*
TOTAL	*$8,333.33*	*$1,811.00*	*$6,522.33*

Fixed expenses

DESCRIPTION	AMOUNT PER MONTH
Rent ($325 per week x 4)	*$1,300.00*
Psychologist ($225 per session x 2)	*$450.00*
Gas bill	*$40.00*
Electricity bill	*$60.00*
Subscriptions (Spotify, Netflix, Binge)	*$47.88*
Health insurance	*$195.00*
Internet	*$60.00*
TOTAL	*$2,102.88*

Monthly budget forecast

EXAMPLE

Complete these pages at the beginning of each month to
forecast what your expenses will be. If you need a refresher,
I run through fixed/necessary expenses and variable/discretionary
expenses in Chapter 2 of *She's on the Money*.

Variable expenses

DESCRIPTION	AMOUNT PER MONTH
Gym classes (6 classes x $25)	$150.00
Pamper allowance (eyelashes & nails)	$200.00
Birthdays x 2 (gift $75 each, dinner x $100)	$250.00
Groceries ($200 per week)	$800.00
TOTAL	**$1,400.00**

Monthly totals

	BUDGETED
TOTAL INCOME	$6,522.33
- TOTAL FIXED EXPENSES	$2,102.88
- TOTAL VARIABLE EXPENSES	$1,400.00
BALANCE	+ $3,019.45

Month 1 budget forecast

Complete these pages at the beginning of each month to
forecast what your expenses will be. If you need a refresher,
I run through fixed/necessary expenses and variable/discretionary
expenses in Chapter 2 of *She's on the Money.*

MONTH:			YEAR:	

Income

SOURCE	GROSS	TAX	NET
TOTAL			

Fixed expenses

DESCRIPTION	AMOUNT PER MONTH
TOTAL	

Month 1 budget forecast

Complete these pages at the beginning of each month to
forecast what your expenses will be. If you need a refresher,
I run through fixed/necessary expenses and variable/discretionary
expenses in Chapter 2 of *She's on the Money*.

Variable expenses

DESCRIPTION	AMOUNT PER MONTH
TOTAL	

Monthly totals

	BUDGETED
TOTAL INCOME	
- TOTAL FIXED EXPENSES	
- TOTAL VARIABLE EXPENSES	
BALANCE	

Daily variable expenses Tracker

Track your variable expenses, such as groceries, dining out and entertainment. On the summary page, you'll group these into categories, which might be worth considering as you log your spending here.

WEEK 1

DATE	DESCRIPTION	TOTAL
	WEEKLY TOTAL	

Daily variable expenses Tracker

Track your variable expenses, such as groceries, dining out and entertainment. On the summary page, you'll group these into categories, which might be worth considering as you log your spending here.

WEEK 2

DATE	DESCRIPTION	TOTAL
	WEEKLY TOTAL	

Daily variable expenses Tracker

Track your variable expenses, such as groceries, dining out and entertainment. On the summary page, you'll group these into categories, which might be worth considering as you log your spending here.

WEEK 3

DATE	DESCRIPTION	TOTAL
	WEEKLY TOTAL	

Daily variable expenses tracker

Track your variable expenses, such as groceries, dining out and entertainment. On the summary page, you'll group these into categories, which might be worth considering as you log your spending here.

WEEK 4

DATE	DESCRIPTION	TOTAL
	WEEKLY TOTAL	

Monthly budget review

Now let's review your month. Based on your daily records, write in the real figures below and compare them with the forecast you wrote at the beginning of the month. Did your spending match what you'd planned? This will be a good time to reflect and re-evaluate for next month.

MONTH: February   **YEAR:** 2023

Income

SOURCE	GROSS	TAX	NET
Salary	$5,833.33	$1,222.00	$4,611.33
Side hustle	$900.00	$195.00	$705.00
TOTAL	$6,733.33	$1,417.00	$5,316.33

Fixed expenses

DESCRIPTION	AMOUNT PER MONTH
Rent ($325 per week x 4)	$1,300.00
Psychologist ($225 per session x 2)	$450.00
Gas bill	$40.00
Electricity bill	$60.00
Subscriptions (Spotify $12.95, Binge $14.95)	$27.90
Health insurance	$145.00
Internet	$60.00
TOTAL	$2,082.90

Monthly budget review

EXAMPLE

Now let's review your month. Based on your daily records, write in the real figures below and compare them with the forecast you wrote at the beginning of the month. Did your spending match what you'd planned? This will be a good time to reflect and re-evaluate for next month.

Variable expenses

DESCRIPTION	AMOUNT PER MONTH
Health & Fitness	$150.00
Personal care/pamper	$180.00
Entertainment/celebrations	$393.00
Groceries	$705.00
Dining out/takeaway	$34.99
Travel	$74.50
TOTAL	$1537.49

Monthly totals

SOURCE	BUDGETED	ACTUAL	DIFFERENCE
TOTAL INCOME	$6,522.33	$5,316.33	– $1,206.00
- TOTAL FIXED EXPENSES	$2,102.88	$2,082.90	$19.98
- TOTAL VARIABLE EXPENSES	$1,400.00	$1,537.49	– $137.49
BALANCE	+ $3,019.45	+ $1,695.94	– $1,323.51

If your actual spending has come in lower than what you budgeted, give some careful thought to how best to use the surplus for your personal goals and situation and refer back to your foolproof cash flow funnel. If it came in higher, can you adjust your spending next month?

Month 1 budget review

Now let's review your month. Based on your daily records, write in the real figures below and compare them with the forecast you wrote at the beginning of the month. Did your spending match what you'd planned? This will be a good time to reflect and re-evaluate for next month.

MONTH:			YEAR:

Income

SOURCE	GROSS	TAX	NET
TOTAL			

Fixed expenses

DESCRIPTION	AMOUNT PER MONTH
TOTAL	

Month 1 budget review

Now let's review your month. Based on your daily records, write in the real figures below and compare them with the forecast you wrote at the beginning of the month. Did your spending match what you'd planned? This will be a good time to reflect and re-evaluate for next month.

Variable expenses

DESCRIPTION	AMOUNT PER MONTH
TOTAL	

Monthly totals

SOURCE	BUDGETED	ACTUAL	DIFFERENCE
TOTAL INCOME			
- TOTAL FIXED EXPENSES			
- TOTAL VARIABLE EXPENSES			
BALANCE			

If your actual spending has come in lower than what you budgeted, give some careful thought to how best to use the surplus for your personal goals and situation and refer back to your foolproof cash-flow funnel. If it came in higher, can you adjust your spending next month?

Notes

Money confession

Money win

Month 1 reflection

To do

Money tip!

Check the *per unit cost* when shopping, as buying larger portions of things you already use regularly (rice, flour, etc.) can save you money in the long run.

Month 2 budget forecast

Complete these pages at the beginning of each month
to forecast what your expenses will be.

MONTH:	YEAR:

Income

SOURCE	GROSS	TAX	NET
TOTAL			

Fixed expenses

DESCRIPTION	AMOUNT PER MONTH
TOTAL	

Month 2 budget forecast

Complete these pages at the beginning of each month
to forecast what your expenses will be.

Variable expenses

DESCRIPTION	AMOUNT PER MONTH
TOTAL	

Monthly totals

	BUDGETED
TOTAL INCOME	
- TOTAL FIXED EXPENSES	
- TOTAL VARIABLE EXPENSES	
BALANCE	

Daily variable expenses Tracker

Track your variable expenses, such as groceries, dining out and entertainment. On the summary page, you'll group these into categories, which might be worth considering as you log your spending here.

WEEK 1

DATE	DESCRIPTION	TOTAL

	WEEKLY TOTAL	

Daily variable expenses tracker

Track your variable expenses, such as groceries, dining out and entertainment. On the summary page, you'll group these into categories, which might be worth considering as you log your spending here.

WEEK 2

DATE	DESCRIPTION	TOTAL
WEEKLY TOTAL		

Daily variable expenses Tracker

Track your variable expenses, such as groceries, dining out and entertainment. On the summary page, you'll group these into categories, which might be worth considering as you log your spending here.

WEEK 3

DATE	DESCRIPTION	TOTAL
WEEKLY TOTAL		

Daily variable expenses Tracker

Track your variable expenses, such as groceries, dining out and entertainment. On the summary page, you'll group these into categories, which might be worth considering as you log your spending here.

DATE	DESCRIPTION	TOTAL
	WEEK 4	
	WEEKLY TOTAL	

Daily variable expenses Tracker

Track your variable expenses, such as groceries, dining out and entertainment. On the summary page, you'll group these into categories, which might be worth considering as you log your spending here.

DATE	DESCRIPTION	TOTAL
	WEEKLY TOTAL	

WEEK 5

Daily variable expenses summary

Now let's group the daily variable expenses you've tracked into categories –
this will help you fill out your monthly budget on the next page.

Variable expenses

CATEGORY	TOTAL COST
Health and fitness	
Personal care/pamper	
Entertainment/celebrations	
Groceries	
Dining out/takeaway	
Travel	
MONTHLY TOTAL	

Month 2 budget review

Now let's review your month. Based on your daily records, write in the real figures below and compare them with the forecast you wrote at the beginning of the month. Did your spending match what you'd planned? This will be a good time to reflect and re-evaluate for next month.

MONTH: **YEAR:**

Income

SOURCE	GROSS	TAX	NET
TOTAL			

Fixed expenses

DESCRIPTION	AMOUNT PER MONTH
TOTAL	

Month 2 budget review

Now let's review your month. Based on your daily records, write in the
real figures below and compare them with the forecast you wrote at the
beginning of the month. Did your spending match what you'd planned?
This will be a good time to reflect and re-evaluate for next month.

Variable expenses

DESCRIPTION	AMOUNT PER MONTH
TOTAL	

Monthly totals

SOURCE	BUDGETED	ACTUAL	DIFFERENCE
TOTAL INCOME			
- TOTAL FIXED EXPENSES			
- TOTAL VARIABLE EXPENSES			
BALANCE			

If your actual spending has come in lower than what you budgeted, give some careful thought to how best
to use the surplus for your personal goals and situation and refer back to your foolproof cash-flow funnel.
If it came in higher, can you adjust your spending next month?

Notes

_____
_____
_____
_____
_____

Money confession

_____
_____
_____
_____
_____
_____

Money win

Month 2 reflection

☐
☐
☐
☐
☐
☐
☐
☐
☐
☐
☐
☐
☐
☐
☐
☐
☐
☐
☐
☐

To do

"

Do it
for
future
you

"

Month 3 budget forecast

Complete these pages at the beginning of each month
to forecast what your expenses will be.

MONTH:	YEAR:

Income

SOURCE	GROSS	TAX	NET
TOTAL			

Fixed expenses

DESCRIPTION	AMOUNT PER MONTH
TOTAL	

Month 3 budget forecast

Complete these pages at the beginning of each month
to forecast what your expenses will be.

Variable expenses

DESCRIPTION	AMOUNT PER MONTH
TOTAL	

Monthly totals

	BUDGETED
TOTAL INCOME	
- TOTAL FIXED EXPENSES	
- TOTAL VARIABLE EXPENSES	
BALANCE	

Daily variable expenses Tracker

Track your variable expenses, such as groceries, dining out and entertainment. On the summary page, you'll group these into categories, which might be worth considering as you log your spending here.

WEEK 1

DATE	DESCRIPTION	TOTAL
	WEEKLY TOTAL	

Daily variable expenses Tracker

Track your variable expenses, such as groceries, dining out and entertainment. On the summary page, you'll group these into categories, which might be worth considering as you log your spending here.

WEEK 2

DATE	DESCRIPTION	TOTAL
	WEEKLY TOTAL	

Daily variable expenses Tracker

Track your variable expenses, such as groceries, dining out and entertainment. On the summary page, you'll group these into categories, which might be worth considering as you log your spending here.

WEEK 3

DATE	DESCRIPTION	TOTAL
	WEEKLY TOTAL	

Daily variable expenses Tracker

Track your variable expenses, such as groceries, dining out and entertainment. On the summary page, you'll group these into categories, which might be worth considering as you log your spending here.

WEEK 4

DATE	DESCRIPTION	TOTAL
	WEEKLY TOTAL	

Daily variable expenses Tracker

Track your variable expenses, such as groceries, dining out and entertainment. On the summary page, you'll group these into categories, which might be worth considering as you log your spending here.

WEEK 5

DATE	DESCRIPTION	TOTAL
	WEEKLY TOTAL	

Daily variable expenses summary

Now let's group the daily variable expenses you've tracked into categories –
this will help you fill out your monthly budget on the next page.

Variable expenses

CATEGORY	TOTAL COST
Health and fitness	
Personal care/pamper	
Entertainment/celebrations	
Groceries	
Dining out/takeaway	
Travel	
MONTHLY TOTAL	

Month 3 budget review

Now let's review your month. Based on your daily records, write in the
real figures below and compare them with the forecast you wrote at the
beginning of the month. Did your spending match what you'd planned?
This will be a good time to reflect and re-evaluate for next month.

MONTH: **YEAR:**

Income

SOURCE	GROSS	TAX	NET
TOTAL			

Fixed expenses

DESCRIPTION	AMOUNT PER MONTH
TOTAL	

Month 3 budget review

Now let's review your month. Based on your daily records, write in the real figures below and compare them with the forecast you wrote at the beginning of the month. Did your spending match what you'd planned? This will be a good time to reflect and re-evaluate for next month.

Variable expenses

DESCRIPTION	AMOUNT PER MONTH
TOTAL	

Monthly totals

SOURCE	BUDGETED	ACTUAL	DIFFERENCE
TOTAL INCOME			
· TOTAL FIXED EXPENSES			
· TOTAL VARIABLE EXPENSES			
BALANCE			

If your actual spending has come in lower than what you budgeted, give some careful thought to how best to use the surplus for your personal goals and situation and refer back to your foolproof cash-flow funnel. If it came in higher, can you adjust your spending next month?

Notes

Money confession

_____

_____

_____

_____

_____

_____

Money win

_____

_____

_____

_____

_____

_____

Month 3 reflection

Quarter 1 reflection

Thinking back on the past three months, take a moment to journal about how you're feeling about your current financial situation.

What do you want to do more of?

_____

_____

What do you want to do less of?

Review your spending on a personal level – are you happy with your spending and does it reflect your values? If you're saving money, are you feeling good about it? Are you allocating enough of your budget to making sure you're enjoying the journey, not just saving it for the destination?

_____

_____

Do you need to set up any direct debits for savings or bills?

_____

_____

Do you need to change the time frame of any of your goals?

_____

_____

- [ ]
- [ ]
- [ ]
- [ ]
- [ ]
- [ ]
- [ ]
- [ ]
- [ ]
- [ ]
- [ ]
- [ ]
- [ ]
- [ ]
- [ ]
- [ ]
- [ ]
- [ ]
- [ ]

To do

Comparison
is the

thief

of joy

Quarter 2

Well done if you're still tracking –
the shine can wear off after the first month or two,
so if you're sticking with it, great job! This is where
the real changes start to happen.

If you're playing along with the 12-month action plan
from the book *She's on the Money*, here are
the next three months' activities.

Month 4: Superannuation

Month 5: Protection and insurances

Month 6: Halfway checkpoint

Month 4 budget forecast

Complete these pages at the beginning of each month
to forecast what your expenses will be.

MONTH:	YEAR:

Income

SOURCE	GROSS	TAX	NET
TOTAL			

Fixed expenses

DESCRIPTION	AMOUNT PER MONTH
TOTAL	

Month 4 budget forecast

Complete these pages at the beginning of each month
to forecast what your expenses will be.

Variable expenses

DESCRIPTION	AMOUNT PER MONTH
TOTAL	

Monthly totals

	BUDGETED
TOTAL INCOME	
- TOTAL FIXED EXPENSES	
- TOTAL VARIABLE EXPENSES	
BALANCE	

Daily variable expenses tracker

Track your variable expenses, such as groceries, dining out and entertainment. On the summary page, you'll group these into categories, which might be worth considering as you log your spending here.

WEEK 1

DATE	DESCRIPTION	TOTAL
	WEEKLY TOTAL	

Daily variable expenses Tracker

Track your variable expenses, such as groceries, dining out and entertainment. On the summary page, you'll group these into categories, which might be worth considering as you log your spending here.

WEEK 2

DATE	DESCRIPTION	TOTAL
	WEEKLY TOTAL	

Daily variable expenses tracker

Track your variable expenses, such as groceries, dining out and entertainment. On the summary page, you'll group these into categories, which might be worth considering as you log your spending here.

WEEK 3

DATE	DESCRIPTION	TOTAL
	WEEKLY TOTAL	

Daily variable expenses tracker

Track your variable expenses, such as groceries, dining out and entertainment. On the summary page, you'll group these into categories, which might be worth considering as you log your spending here.

WEEK 4

DATE	DESCRIPTION	TOTAL
	WEEKLY TOTAL	

Daily variable expenses Tracker

Track your variable expenses, such as groceries, dining out and entertainment. On the summary page, you'll group these into categories, which might be worth considering as you log your spending here.

WEEK 5

DATE	DESCRIPTION	TOTAL
WEEKLY TOTAL		

Daily variable expenses summary

Now let's group the daily variable expenses you've tracked into categories –
this will help you fill out your monthly budget on the next page.

Variable expenses

CATEGORY	TOTAL COST
Health and fitness	
Personal care/pamper	
Entertainment/celebrations	
Groceries	
Dining out/takeaway	
Travel	
MONTHLY TOTAL	

Month 4 budget review

Now let's review your month. Based on your daily records, write in the real figures below and compare them with the forecast you wrote at the beginning of the month. Did your spending match what you'd planned? This will be a good time to reflect and re-evaluate for next month.

MONTH: **YEAR:**

Income

SOURCE	GROSS	TAX	NET
TOTAL			

Fixed expenses

DESCRIPTION	AMOUNT PER MONTH
TOTAL	

Month 4 budget review

Now let's review your month. Based on your daily records, write in the real figures below and compare them with the forecast you wrote at the beginning of the month. Did your spending match what you'd planned? This will be a good time to reflect and re-evaluate for next month.

Variable expenses

DESCRIPTION	AMOUNT PER MONTH
TOTAL	

Monthly totals

SOURCE	BUDGETED	ACTUAL	DIFFERENCE
TOTAL INCOME			
· TOTAL FIXED EXPENSES			
· TOTAL VARIABLE EXPENSES			
BALANCE			

If your actual spending has come in lower than what you budgeted, give some careful thought to how best to use the surplus for your personal goals and situation and refer back to your foolproof cash-flow funnel. If it came in higher, can you adjust your spending next month?

Notes

Money confession

Money win

Month 4 reflection

To do

- [ ]
- [ ]
- [ ]
- [ ]
- [ ]
- [ ]
- [ ]
- [ ]
- [ ]
- [ ]
- [ ]
- [ ]
- [ ]
- [ ]
- [ ]
- [ ]
- [ ]
- [ ]

Challenge!

Declutter one room in your house and sell, donate or give away three items.

Month 5 budget forecast

Complete these pages at the beginning of each month
to forecast what your expenses will be.

MONTH: **YEAR:**

Income

SOURCE	GROSS	TAX	NET
TOTAL			

Fixed expenses

DESCRIPTION	AMOUNT PER MONTH
TOTAL	

Month 5 budget forecast

Complete these pages at the beginning of each month
to forecast what your expenses will be.

Variable expenses

DESCRIPTION	AMOUNT PER MONTH
TOTAL	

Monthly totals

	BUDGETED
TOTAL INCOME	
- TOTAL FIXED EXPENSES	
- TOTAL VARIABLE EXPENSES	
BALANCE	

Daily variable expenses tracker

Track your variable expenses, such as groceries, dining out and entertainment. On the summary page, you'll group these into categories, which might be worth considering as you log your spending here.

WEEK 1		
DATE	DESCRIPTION	TOTAL
	WEEKLY TOTAL	

Daily variable expenses tracker

Track your variable expenses, such as groceries, dining out and entertainment. On the summary page, you'll group these into categories, which might be worth considering as you log your spending here.

WEEK 2

DATE	DESCRIPTION	TOTAL
WEEKLY TOTAL		

Daily variable expenses tracker

Track your variable expenses, such as groceries, dining out and entertainment. On the summary page, you'll group these into categories, which might be worth considering as you log your spending here.

WEEK 3

DATE	DESCRIPTION	TOTAL
	WEEKLY TOTAL	

Daily variable expenses Tracker

Track your variable expenses, such as groceries, dining out and entertainment. On the summary page, you'll group these into categories, which might be worth considering as you log your spending here.

WEEK 4

DATE	DESCRIPTION	TOTAL
	WEEKLY TOTAL	

Daily variable expenses tracker

Track your variable expenses, such as groceries, dining out and entertainment. On the summary page, you'll group these into categories, which might be worth considering as you log your spending here.

WEEK 5

DATE	DESCRIPTION	TOTAL
	WEEKLY TOTAL	

Daily variable expenses summary

Now let's group the daily variable expenses you've tracked into categories –
this will help you fill out your monthly budget on the next page.

Variable expenses

CATEGORY	TOTAL COST
Health and fitness	
Personal care/pamper	
Entertainment/celebrations	
Groceries	
Dining out/takeaway	
Travel	
MONTHLY TOTAL	

Month's budget review

Now let's review your month. Based on your daily records, write in the real figures below and compare them with the forecast you wrote at the beginning of the month. Did your spending match what you'd planned? This will be a good time to reflect and re-evaluate for next month.

| MONTH: | | | YEAR: |

Income

SOURCE	GROSS	TAX	NET
TOTAL			

Fixed expenses

DESCRIPTION	AMOUNT PER MONTH
TOTAL	

Month 5 budget review

Now let's review your month. Based on your daily records, write in the real figures below and compare them with the forecast you wrote at the beginning of the month. Did your spending match what you'd planned? This will be a good time to reflect and re-evaluate for next month.

Variable expenses

DESCRIPTION	AMOUNT PER MONTH
TOTAL	

Monthly totals

SOURCE	BUDGETED	ACTUAL	DIFFERENCE
TOTAL INCOME			
· TOTAL FIXED EXPENSES			
· TOTAL VARIABLE EXPENSES			
BALANCE			

If your actual spending has come in lower than what you budgeted, give some careful thought to how best to use the surplus for your personal goals and situation and refer back to your foolproof cash-flow funnel. If it came in higher, can you adjust your spending next month?

Notes

Month 5 reflection

Money win

Money confession

To do

- [ ]
- [ ]
- [ ]
- [ ]
- [ ]
- [ ]
- [ ]
- [ ]
- [ ]
- [ ]
- [ ]
- [ ]
- [ ]
- [ ]
- [ ]
- [ ]
- [ ]
- [ ]

Challenge!

This week,
'shop' your pantry!
Only use items that you've
already purchased.

Month 6 budget forecast

Complete these pages at the beginning of each month
to forecast what your expenses will be.

MONTH:	YEAR:

Income

SOURCE	GROSS	TAX	NET
TOTAL			

Fixed expenses

DESCRIPTION	AMOUNT PER MONTH
TOTAL	

Month 6 budget forecast

Complete these pages at the beginning of each month
to forecast what your expenses will be.

Variable expenses

DESCRIPTION	AMOUNT PER MONTH
TOTAL	

Monthly totals

	BUDGETED
TOTAL INCOME	
- TOTAL FIXED EXPENSES	
- TOTAL VARIABLE EXPENSES	
BALANCE	

Daily variable expenses tracker

Track your variable expenses, such as groceries, dining out and entertainment. On the summary page, you'll group these into categories, which might be worth considering as you log your spending here.

WEEK 1

DATE	DESCRIPTION	TOTAL
	WEEKLY TOTAL	

Daily variable expenses tracker

Track your variable expenses, such as groceries, dining out and entertainment. On the summary page, you'll group these into categories, which might be worth considering as you log your spending here.

WEEK 2

DATE	DESCRIPTION	TOTAL
	WEEKLY TOTAL	

Daily variable expenses tracker

Track your variable expenses, such as groceries, dining out and entertainment. On the summary page, you'll group these into categories, which might be worth considering as you log your spending here.

WEEK 3

DATE	DESCRIPTION	TOTAL
	WEEKLY TOTAL	

Daily variable expenses Tracker

Track your variable expenses, such as groceries, dining out and entertainment. On the summary page, you'll group these into categories, which might be worth considering as you log your spending here.

WEEK 4

DATE	DESCRIPTION	TOTAL
	WEEKLY TOTAL	

Daily variable expenses Tracker

Track your variable expenses, such as groceries, dining out and entertainment. On the summary page, you'll group these into categories, which might be worth considering as you log your spending here.

WEEK 5

DATE	DESCRIPTION	TOTAL

WEEKLY TOTAL	

Daily variable expenses summary

Now let's group the daily variable expenses you've tracked into categories –
this will help you fill out your monthly budget on the next page.

Variable expenses

CATEGORY	TOTAL COST
Health and fitness	
Personal care/pamper	
Entertainment/celebrations	
Groceries	
Dining out/takeaway	
Travel	
MONTHLY TOTAL	

Month 6 budget review

Now let's review your month. Based on your daily records, write in the real figures below and compare them with the forecast you wrote at the beginning of the month. Did your spending match what you'd planned? This will be a good time to reflect and re-evaluate for next month.

| MONTH: | | | YEAR: |

Income

SOURCE	GROSS	TAX	NET
TOTAL			

Fixed expenses

DESCRIPTION	AMOUNT PER MONTH
TOTAL	

Month 6 budget review

Now let's review your month. Based on your daily records, write in the real figures below and compare them with the forecast you wrote at the beginning of the month. Did your spending match what you'd planned? This will be a good time to reflect and re-evaluate for next month.

Variable expenses

DESCRIPTION	AMOUNT PER MONTH
TOTAL	

Monthly totals

SOURCE	BUDGETED	ACTUAL	DIFFERENCE
TOTAL INCOME			
· TOTAL FIXED EXPENSES			
· TOTAL VARIABLE EXPENSES			
BALANCE			

If your actual spending has come in lower than what you budgeted, give some careful thought to how best to use the surplus for your personal goals and situation and refer back to your foolproof cash-flow funnel. If it came in higher, can you adjust your spending next month?

Notes

Month 6 reflection

Money win

_____
_____
_____
_____
_____
_____

Money confession

_____
_____
_____
_____
_____
_____

Quarter 2 reflection

Thinking back on the past three months, take a moment to journal about how you're feeling about your current financial situation.

What do you want to do more of?

_____

_____

What do you want to do less of?

Review your spending on a personal level – are you happy with your spending and does it reflect your values? If you're saving money, are you feeling good about it? Are you allocating enough of your budget to making sure you're enjoying the journey, not just saving it for the destination?

_____

_____

Do you need to set up any direct debits for savings or bills?

_____

_____

Do you need to change the time frame of any of your goals?

_____

_____

☐

☐

☐

☐

☐

☐

☐

☐

☐

☐

☐

☐

☐

☐

☐

☐

☐

☐

☐

To do

Money Tip!

Libraries are a great way to access cheap or *free entertainment* with availability to loan books, movies, magazines and more. Sometimes, they even hold events!

Quarter 3

Congratulations, you've reached the halfway point! Now's a good time to check in on your progress for your financial goals, especially the short-term and medium-term ones.

If you're playing along with the 12-month action plan from the book *She's on the Money*, here are the next three months' activities.

Month 7: Self-care

Month 8: Estate planning

Month 9: Double down on debt/ramp up your savings

Month 7 budget forecast

Complete these pages at the beginning of each month
to forecast what your expenses will be.

MONTH:	YEAR:

Income

SOURCE	GROSS	TAX	NET
TOTAL			

Fixed expenses

DESCRIPTION	AMOUNT PER MONTH
TOTAL	

Month 7 budget forecast

Complete these pages at the beginning of each month
to forecast what your expenses will be.

Variable expenses

DESCRIPTION	AMOUNT PER MONTH
TOTAL	

Monthly totals

	BUDGETED
TOTAL INCOME	
- TOTAL FIXED EXPENSES	
- TOTAL VARIABLE EXPENSES	
BALANCE	

Daily variable expenses Tracker

Track your variable expenses, such as groceries, dining out and entertainment. On the summary page, you'll group these into categories, which might be worth considering as you log your spending here.

WEEK 1

DATE	DESCRIPTION	TOTAL
	WEEKLY TOTAL	

Daily variable expenses Tracker

Track your variable expenses, such as groceries, dining out and entertainment. On the summary page, you'll group these into categories, which might be worth considering as you log your spending here.

WEEK 2

DATE	DESCRIPTION	TOTAL
	WEEKLY TOTAL	

Daily variable expenses Tracker

Track your variable expenses, such as groceries, dining out and entertainment. On the summary page, you'll group these into categories, which might be worth considering as you log your spending here.

WEEK 3

DATE	DESCRIPTION	TOTAL
	WEEKLY TOTAL	

Daily variable expenses tracker

Track your variable expenses, such as groceries, dining out and entertainment. On the summary page, you'll group these into categories, which might be worth considering as you log your spending here.

WEEK 4

DATE	DESCRIPTION	TOTAL
	WEEKLY TOTAL	

Daily variable expenses tracker

Track your variable expenses, such as groceries, dining out and entertainment. On the summary page, you'll group these into categories, which might be worth considering as you log your spending here.

WEEK 5

DATE	DESCRIPTION	TOTAL
	WEEKLY TOTAL	

Daily variable expenses summary

Now let's group the daily variable expenses you've tracked into categories –
this will help you fill out your monthly budget on the next page.

Variable expenses

CATEGORY	TOTAL COST
Health and fitness	
Personal care/pamper	
Entertainment/celebrations	
Groceries	
Dining out/takeaway	
Travel	
MONTHLY TOTAL	

Month 7 budget review

Now let's review your month. Based on your daily records, write in the real figures below and compare them with the forecast you wrote at the beginning of the month. Did your spending match what you'd planned? This will be a good time to reflect and re-evaluate for next month.

MONTH:

YEAR:

Income

SOURCE	GROSS	TAX	NET
TOTAL			

Fixed expenses

DESCRIPTION	AMOUNT PER MONTH
TOTAL	

Month 7 budget review

Now let's review your month. Based on your daily records, write in the real figures below and compare them with the forecast you wrote at the beginning of the month. Did your spending match what you'd planned? This will be a good time to reflect and re-evaluate for next month.

Variable expenses

DESCRIPTION	AMOUNT PER MONTH
TOTAL	

Monthly totals

SOURCE	BUDGETED	ACTUAL	DIFFERENCE
TOTAL INCOME			
- TOTAL FIXED EXPENSES			
- TOTAL VARIABLE EXPENSES			
BALANCE			

If your actual spending has come in lower than what you budgeted, give some careful thought to how best to use the surplus for your personal goals and situation and refer back to your foolproof cash-flow funnel. If it came in higher, can you adjust your spending next month?

Notes

Money confession

Money win

Month 7 reflection

To do

- [ ]
- [ ]
- [ ]
- [ ]
- [ ]
- [ ]
- [ ]
- [ ]
- [ ]
- [ ]
- [ ]
- [ ]
- [ ]
- [ ]
- [ ]
- [ ]
- [ ]
- [ ]

Money Tip!

Buy a water bottle that you like and have a reminder to *fill it up* at home before heading out.

This will help you save money while also reducing the environmental impact of single-use plastic.

NEW MONTH

Month 8 budget forecast

Complete these pages at the beginning of each month
to forecast what your expenses will be.

Income

SOURCE	GROSS	TAX	NET
TOTAL			

Fixed expenses

DESCRIPTION	AMOUNT PER MONTH
TOTAL	

Month 8 budget forecast

Complete these pages at the beginning of each month
to forecast what your expenses will be.

Variable expenses

DESCRIPTION	AMOUNT PER MONTH
TOTAL	

Monthly totals

	BUDGETED
TOTAL INCOME	
- TOTAL FIXED EXPENSES	
- TOTAL VARIABLE EXPENSES	
BALANCE	

Daily variable expenses Tracker

Track your variable expenses, such as groceries, dining out and entertainment. On the summary page, you'll group these into categories, which might be worth considering as you log your spending here.

WEEK 1

DATE	DESCRIPTION	TOTAL
	WEEKLY TOTAL	

Daily variable expenses tracker

Track your variable expenses, such as groceries, dining out and entertainment. On the summary page, you'll group these into categories, which might be worth considering as you log your spending here.

WEEK 2

DATE	DESCRIPTION	TOTAL
	WEEKLY TOTAL	

Daily variable expenses tracker

Track your variable expenses, such as groceries, dining out and entertainment. On the summary page, you'll group these into categories, which might be worth considering as you log your spending here.

WEEK 3

DATE	DESCRIPTION	TOTAL
	WEEKLY TOTAL	

Daily variable expenses tracker

Track your variable expenses, such as groceries, dining out and entertainment. On the summary page, you'll group these into categories, which might be worth considering as you log your spending here.

WEEK 4

DATE	DESCRIPTION	TOTAL
WEEKLY TOTAL		

Daily variable expenses tracker

Track your variable expenses, such as groceries, dining out and entertainment. On the summary page, you'll group these into categories, which might be worth considering as you log your spending here.

WEEK 5

DATE	DESCRIPTION	TOTAL
	WEEKLY TOTAL	

Daily variable expenses summary

Now let's group the daily variable expenses you've tracked into categories –
this will help you fill out your monthly budget on the next page.

Variable expenses

CATEGORY	TOTAL COST
Health and fitness	
Personal care/pamper	
Entertainment/celebrations	
Groceries	
Dining out/takeaway	
Travel	
MONTHLY TOTAL	

Month 8 budget review

Now let's review your month. Based on your daily records, write in the real figures below and compare them with the forecast you wrote at the beginning of the month. Did your spending match what you'd planned? This will be a good time to reflect and re-evaluate for next month.

MONTH:

YEAR:

Income

SOURCE	GROSS	TAX	NET
TOTAL			

Fixed expenses

DESCRIPTION	AMOUNT PER MONTH
TOTAL	

Month 8 budget review

Now let's review your month. Based on your daily records, write in the real figures below and compare them with the forecast you wrote at the beginning of the month. Did your spending match what you'd planned? This will be a good time to reflect and re-evaluate for next month.

Variable expenses

DESCRIPTION	AMOUNT PER MONTH
TOTAL	

Monthly totals

SOURCE	BUDGETED	ACTUAL	DIFFERENCE
TOTAL INCOME			
- TOTAL FIXED EXPENSES			
- TOTAL VARIABLE EXPENSES			
BALANCE			

If your actual spending has come in lower than what you budgeted, give some careful thought to how best to use the surplus for your personal goals and situation and refer back to your foolproof cash-flow funnel. If it came in higher, can you adjust your spending next month?

Notes

Money confession

Money win

Month 8 reflection

To do

- [ ]
- [ ]
- [ ]
- [ ]
- [ ]
- [ ]
- [ ]
- [ ]
- [ ]
- [ ]
- [ ]
- [ ]
- [ ]
- [ ]
- [ ]
- [ ]
- [ ]
- [ ]

Challenge!

Plan a *date night* that's 100% free!

Make it a competition between yourself and your partner (or your friends) to see who can design the best free date night and do it!

Month 9 budget forecast

Complete these pages at the beginning of each month
to forecast what your expenses will be.

MONTH: **YEAR:**

Income

SOURCE	GROSS	TAX	NET
TOTAL			

Fixed expenses

DESCRIPTION	AMOUNT PER MONTH
TOTAL	

Month 9 budget forecast

Complete these pages at the beginning of each month
to forecast what your expenses will be.

Variable expenses

DESCRIPTION	AMOUNT PER MONTH
TOTAL	

Monthly totals

	BUDGETED
TOTAL INCOME	
- TOTAL FIXED EXPENSES	
- TOTAL VARIABLE EXPENSES	
BALANCE	

Daily variable expenses tracker

Track your variable expenses, such as groceries, dining out and entertainment. On the summary page, you'll group these into categories, which might be worth considering as you log your spending here.

WEEK 1

DATE	DESCRIPTION	TOTAL
	WEEKLY TOTAL	

Daily variable expenses tracker

Track your variable expenses, such as groceries, dining out and entertainment. On the summary page, you'll group these into categories, which might be worth considering as you log your spending here.

WEEK 2

DATE	DESCRIPTION	TOTAL
	WEEKLY TOTAL	

Daily variable expenses tracker

Track your variable expenses, such as groceries, dining out and entertainment. On the summary page, you'll group these into categories, which might be worth considering as you log your spending here.

WEEK 3

DATE	DESCRIPTION	TOTAL
	WEEKLY TOTAL	

Daily variable expenses Tracker

Track your variable expenses, such as groceries, dining out and entertainment. On the summary page, you'll group these into categories, which might be worth considering as you log your spending here.

WEEK 4

DATE	DESCRIPTION	TOTAL
	WEEKLY TOTAL	

Daily variable expenses tracker

Track your variable expenses, such as groceries, dining out and entertainment. On the summary page, you'll group these into categories, which might be worth considering as you log your spending here.

WEEK 5

DATE	DESCRIPTION	TOTAL
	WEEKLY TOTAL	

Daily variable expenses summary

Now let's group the daily variable expenses you've tracked into categories –
this will help you fill out your monthly budget on the next page.

Variable expenses

CATEGORY	TOTAL COST
Health and fitness	
Personal care/pamper	
Entertainment/celebrations	
Groceries	
Dining out/takeaway	
Travel	
MONTHLY TOTAL	

Month 9 budget review

Now let's review your month. Based on your daily records, write in the real figures below and compare them with the forecast you wrote at the beginning of the month. Did your spending match what you'd planned? This will be a good time to reflect and re-evaluate for next month.

Income

SOURCE	GROSS	TAX	NET
TOTAL			

Fixed expenses

DESCRIPTION	AMOUNT PER MONTH
TOTAL	

Month 9 budget review

Now let's review your month. Based on your daily records, write in the real figures below and compare them with the forecast you wrote at the beginning of the month. Did your spending match what you'd planned? This will be a good time to reflect and re-evaluate for next month.

Variable expenses

DESCRIPTION	AMOUNT PER MONTH
TOTAL	

Monthly totals

SOURCE	BUDGETED	ACTUAL	DIFFERENCE
TOTAL INCOME			
· TOTAL FIXED EXPENSES			
· TOTAL VARIABLE EXPENSES			
BALANCE			

If your actual spending has come in lower than what you budgeted, give some careful thought to how best to use the surplus for your personal goals and situation and refer back to your foolproof cash-flow funnel. If it came in higher, can you adjust your spending next month?

Notes

Month 9 reflection

Money win

Money confession

Quarter 3 reflection

Thinking back on the past three months, take a moment to journal about how you're feeling about your current financial situation.

What do you want to do more of?

What do you want to do less of?

Review your spending on a personal level – are you happy with your spending and does it reflect your values? If you're saving money, are you feeling good about it? Are you allocating enough of your budget to making sure you're enjoying the journey, not just saving it for the destination?

Do you need to set up any direct debits for savings or bills?

Do you need to change the time frame of any of your goals?

To do

"

You're one
in a

million

(dollars)

"

Quarter 4

Three-quarters of the year down, one to go. What tweaks can you make to your goals to ensure you hit your targets?

If you're playing along with the 12-month action plan from the book *She's on the Money*, here are the final three months' activities.

Month 10: Continuing education

Month 11: Spending detox

Month 12: Celebrate!

Month 10 budget forecast

Complete these pages at the beginning of each month
to forecast what your expenses will be.

MONTH: **YEAR:**

Income

SOURCE	GROSS	TAX	NET
TOTAL			

Fixed expenses

DESCRIPTION	AMOUNT PER MONTH
TOTAL	

Month 10 budget forecast

Complete these pages at the beginning of each month
to forecast what your expenses will be.

Variable expenses

DESCRIPTION	AMOUNT PER MONTH
TOTAL	

Monthly totals

	BUDGETED
TOTAL INCOME	
- TOTAL FIXED EXPENSES	
- TOTAL VARIABLE EXPENSES	
BALANCE	

Daily variable expenses Tracker

Track your variable expenses, such as groceries, dining out and entertainment. On the summary page, you'll group these into categories, which might be worth considering as you log your spending here.

WEEK 1

DATE	DESCRIPTION	TOTAL
	WEEKLY TOTAL	

Daily variable expenses tracker

Track your variable expenses, such as groceries, dining out and entertainment. On the summary page, you'll group these into categories, which might be worth considering as you log your spending here.

WEEK 2

DATE	DESCRIPTION	TOTAL
	WEEKLY TOTAL	

Daily variable expenses tracker

Track your variable expenses, such as groceries, dining out and entertainment. On the summary page, you'll group these into categories, which might be worth considering as you log your spending here.

WEEK 3

DATE	DESCRIPTION	TOTAL
	WEEKLY TOTAL	

Daily variable expenses Tracker

Track your variable expenses, such as groceries, dining out and entertainment. On the summary page, you'll group these into categories, which might be worth considering as you log your spending here.

WEEK 4

DATE	DESCRIPTION	TOTAL
	WEEKLY TOTAL	

Daily variable expenses tracker

Track your variable expenses, such as groceries, dining out and entertainment. On the summary page, you'll group these into categories, which might be worth considering as you log your spending here.

WEEK 5

DATE	DESCRIPTION	TOTAL
	WEEKLY TOTAL	

Daily variable expenses summary

Now let's group the daily variable expenses you've tracked into categories –
this will help you fill out your monthly budget on the next page.

Variable expenses

CATEGORY	TOTAL COST
Health and fitness	
Personal care/pamper	
Entertainment/celebrations	
Groceries	
Dining out/takeaway	
Travel	
MONTHLY TOTAL	

Month 10 budget review

Now let's review your month. Based on your daily records, write in the
real figures below and compare them with the forecast you wrote at the
beginning of the month. Did your spending match what you'd planned?
This will be a good time to reflect and re-evaluate for next month.

MONTH:	YEAR:

Income

SOURCE	GROSS	TAX	NET
TOTAL			

Fixed expenses

DESCRIPTION	AMOUNT PER MONTH
TOTAL	

Month 10 budget review

Now let's review your month. Based on your daily records, write in the real figures below and compare them with the forecast you wrote at the beginning of the month. Did your spending match what you'd planned? This will be a good time to reflect and re-evaluate for next month.

Variable expenses

DESCRIPTION	AMOUNT PER MONTH
TOTAL	

Monthly totals

SOURCE	BUDGETED	ACTUAL	DIFFERENCE
TOTAL INCOME			
· TOTAL FIXED EXPENSES			
· TOTAL VARIABLE EXPENSES			
BALANCE			

If your actual spending has come in lower than what you budgeted, give some careful thought to how best to use the surplus for your personal goals and situation and refer back to your foolproof cash-flow funnel. If it came in higher, can you adjust your spending next month?

Notes

Month 10 reflection

Money win

Money confession

To do

- [ ] _____
- [ ] _____
- [ ] _____
- [ ] _____
- [ ] _____
- [ ] _____
- [ ] _____
- [ ] _____
- [ ] _____
- [ ] _____
- [ ] _____
- [ ] _____
- [ ] _____
- [ ] _____
- [ ] _____
- [ ] _____
- [ ] _____
- [ ] _____

"

language

love

is my

Investing
"

Month 11 budget forecast

Complete these pages at the beginning of each month
to forecast what your expenses will be.

MONTH: **YEAR:**

Income

SOURCE	GROSS	TAX	NET
TOTAL			

Fixed expenses

DESCRIPTION	AMOUNT PER MONTH
TOTAL	

Month 11 budget forecast

Complete these pages at the beginning of each month
to forecast what your expenses will be.

Variable expenses

DESCRIPTION	AMOUNT PER MONTH
TOTAL	

Monthly totals

	BUDGETED
TOTAL INCOME	
- TOTAL FIXED EXPENSES	
- TOTAL VARIABLE EXPENSES	
BALANCE	

Daily variable expenses Tracker

Track your variable expenses, such as groceries, dining out and entertainment. On the summary page, you'll group these into categories, which might be worth considering as you log your spending here.

WEEK 1

DATE	DESCRIPTION	TOTAL
	WEEKLY TOTAL	

Daily variable expenses Tracker

Track your variable expenses, such as groceries, dining out and entertainment. On the summary page, you'll group these into categories, which might be worth considering as you log your spending here.

WEEK 2

DATE	DESCRIPTION	TOTAL
	WEEKLY TOTAL	

Daily variable expenses tracker

Track your variable expenses, such as groceries, dining out and entertainment. On the summary page, you'll group these into categories, which might be worth considering as you log your spending here.

WEEK 3

DATE	DESCRIPTION	TOTAL
	WEEKLY TOTAL	

Daily variable expenses tracker

Track your variable expenses, such as groceries, dining out and entertainment. On the summary page, you'll group these into categories, which might be worth considering as you log your spending here.

DATE	DESCRIPTION	TOTAL
	WEEKLY TOTAL	

Daily variable expenses tracker

Track your variable expenses, such as groceries, dining out and entertainment. On the summary page, you'll group these into categories, which might be worth considering as you log your spending here.

WEEK 5

DATE	DESCRIPTION	TOTAL
	WEEKLY TOTAL	

Daily variable expenses summary

Now let's group the daily variable expenses you've tracked into categories –
this will help you fill out your monthly budget on the next page.

Variable expenses

CATEGORY	TOTAL COST
Health and fitness	
Personal care/pamper	
Entertainment/celebrations	
Groceries	
Dining out/takeaway	
Travel	
MONTHLY TOTAL	

Month 11 budget review

Now let's review your month. Based on your daily records, write in the real figures below and compare them with the forecast you wrote at the beginning of the month. Did your spending match what you'd planned? This will be a good time to reflect and re-evaluate for next month.

MONTH: **YEAR:**

Income

SOURCE	GROSS	TAX	NET
TOTAL			

Fixed expenses

DESCRIPTION	AMOUNT PER MONTH
TOTAL	

Month 11 budget review

Now let's review your month. Based on your daily records, write in the real figures below and compare them with the forecast you wrote at the beginning of the month. Did your spending match what you'd planned? This will be a good time to reflect and re-evaluate for next month.

Variable expenses

DESCRIPTION	AMOUNT PER MONTH
TOTAL	

Monthly totals

SOURCE	BUDGETED	ACTUAL	DIFFERENCE
TOTAL INCOME			
· TOTAL FIXED EXPENSES			
· TOTAL VARIABLE EXPENSES			
BALANCE			

If your actual spending has come in lower than what you budgeted, give some careful thought to how best to use the surplus for your personal goals and situation and refer back to your foolproof cash-flow funnel. If it came in higher, can you adjust your spending next month?

Notes

Month 11 reflection

Money win

_____
_____
_____
_____
_____
_____
_____

Money confession

_____
_____
_____
_____
_____

To do

Challenge!

Transfer $30 into

your savings account

right now!

(if you can)

Month 12 budget forecast

Complete these pages at the beginning of each month
to forecast what your expenses will be.

MONTH:		YEAR:	

Income

SOURCE	GROSS	TAX	NET
TOTAL			

Fixed expenses

DESCRIPTION	AMOUNT PER MONTH
TOTAL	

Month 12 budget forecast

Complete these pages at the beginning of each month
to forecast what your expenses will be.

Variable expenses

DESCRIPTION	AMOUNT PER MONTH
TOTAL	

Monthly totals

	BUDGETED
TOTAL INCOME	
- TOTAL FIXED EXPENSES	
- TOTAL VARIABLE EXPENSES	
BALANCE	

Daily variable expenses Tracker

Track your variable expenses, such as groceries, dining out and entertainment. On the summary page, you'll group these into categories, which might be worth considering as you log your spending here.

WEEK 1

DATE	DESCRIPTION	TOTAL
WEEKLY TOTAL		

Daily variable expenses Tracker

Track your variable expenses, such as groceries, dining out and entertainment. On the summary page, you'll group these into categories, which might be worth considering as you log your spending here.

WEEK 2

DATE	DESCRIPTION	TOTAL
WEEKLY TOTAL		

Daily variable expenses Tracker

Track your variable expenses, such as groceries, dining out and entertainment. On the summary page, you'll group these into categories, which might be worth considering as you log your spending here.

WEEK 3		
DATE	DESCRIPTION	TOTAL
WEEKLY TOTAL		

Daily variable expenses Tracker

Track your variable expenses, such as groceries, dining out and entertainment. On the summary page, you'll group these into categories, which might be worth considering as you log your spending here.

DATE	DESCRIPTION	TOTAL
	WEEKLY TOTAL	

Daily variable expenses tracker

Track your variable expenses, such as groceries, dining out and entertainment. On the summary page, you'll group these into categories, which might be worth considering as you log your spending here.

WEEK 5

DATE	DESCRIPTION	TOTAL
	WEEKLY TOTAL	

Daily variable expenses summary

Now let's group the daily variable expenses you've tracked into categories –
this will help you fill out your monthly budget on the next page.

Variable expenses

CATEGORY	TOTAL COST
Health and fitness	
Personal care/pamper	
Entertainment/celebrations	
Groceries	
Dining out/takeaway	
Travel	
MONTHLY TOTAL	

Month 12 budget review

Now let's review your month. Based on your daily records, write in the
real figures below and compare them with the forecast you wrote at the
beginning of the month. Did your spending match what you'd planned?
This will be a good time to reflect and re-evaluate for next month.

MONTH: **YEAR:**

Income

SOURCE	GROSS	TAX	NET
TOTAL			

Fixed expenses

DESCRIPTION	AMOUNT PER MONTH
TOTAL	

Month 12 budget review

Now let's review your month. Based on your daily records, write in the real figures below and compare them with the forecast you wrote at the beginning of the month. Did your spending match what you'd planned? This will be a good time to reflect and re-evaluate for next month.

Variable expenses

DESCRIPTION	AMOUNT PER MONTH
TOTAL	

Monthly totals

SOURCE	BUDGETED	ACTUAL	DIFFERENCE
TOTAL INCOME			
· TOTAL FIXED EXPENSES			
· TOTAL VARIABLE EXPENSES			
BALANCE			

If your actual spending has come in lower than what you budgeted, give some careful thought to how best to use the surplus for your personal goals and situation and refer back to your foolproof cash-flow funnel. If it came in higher, can you adjust your spending next month?

Notes

Month 12 reflection

Money win

Money confession

Quarter 4 reflection

Thinking back on the past three months, take a moment to journal about how you're feeling about your current financial situation.

What do you want to do more of?

_____

_____

What do you want to do less of?

_____

_____

Review your spending on a personal level – are you happy with your spending and does it reflect your values? If you're saving money, are you feeling good about it? Are you allocating enough of your budget to making sure you're enjoying the journey, not just saving it for the destination?

Do you need to set up any direct debits for savings or bills?

_____

_____

Do you need to change the time frame of any of your goals?

_____

_____

To do

Money tip!

Utilise your bank's
round-up feature.

Most banks offer round-ups as an optional feature.
Each time you make a purchase, the amount withdrawn is
rounded up to a set figure (often the nearest dollar),
with the difference being transferred to your savings account.
This is a great way to save without even noticing!

Year in review

You made it!

Congratulations on making your financial health
a priority this year. I hope the tools, tips and resources
in this journal have helped make it an enjoyable
learning experience.

In this section you'll compare your results with
the goals you set up at the start to see what worked and
what didn't. Remember, no matter the outcome, it is all
an opportunity to learn from your efforts and continue
making progress towards Future You. Just imagine what's
around the corner if you keep taking these positive
steps in your money habits.

Take a moment to celebrate your successes
(within budget, of course!) and then it's time for
a new *She's on the Money Budget Journal*, to start fresh.

Long-term goal review

Congratulations on making it to the end of the year! Now, look back on the long-term goal you set at the start of this 12-month journey and see how you're tracking. What's been a win along the way? How could you improve?

Money win

Money confession

Medium-term goals review

At the beginning of the year, you set two medium-term goals.
Review your progress here. You still have time to change tack and meet your
3–5 year dream, so look carefully and see what might need adjusting.

Money win

_____

_____

_____

_____

_____

Money confession

_____

_____

_____

_____

_____

Short-term goals review

At the beginning of the year you set two short-term goals to achieve over the 12 months. How did you go? What worked and what didn't – what might you improve next year?

Money win

_____

_____

_____

_____

_____

Money confession

_____

_____

_____

_____

_____

Do you need to change the specifics of any of your goals?

Consider your goals' reviews on the previous pages. Where are you gaining or losing? Do you need to adjust your budgets to get closer to Future You? If this journal worked for you, now's the time to pick up a fresh one for next year and set some new goals for the next 12 months.

_____

_____

What do you want to do less of?

_____

What do you want to do more of?

_____

What were the financial highlights?

It's been a big year. Let's take a moment to reflect on your 12-month financial journey.

_____

year in review

Notes

_____

_____

_____

_____

_____

_____

_____

_____

_____

_____

_____

_____

_____

_____

_____

_____

_____

_____

_____

_____

_____

_____

_____

_____

_____

Notes

Notes

☐
☐
☐
☐
☐
☐
☐
☐
☐
☐
☐
☐
☐
☐
☐
☐
☐
☐
☐
☐

To do

To do

- [ ]
- [ ]
- [ ]
- [ ]
- [ ]
- [ ]
- [ ]
- [ ]
- [ ]
- [ ]
- [ ]
- [ ]
- [ ]
- [ ]
- [ ]
- [ ]
- [ ]
- [ ]
- [ ]

To do

"

More money

=

more freedom

"